The Dream Journal

Track Your Dreams and Work Out What They Mean

ANNA BARNES

summersdale

THE DREAM JOURNAL

An Hachette UK Company
www.hachette.co.uk

Summersdale Publishers Ltd
Part of Octopus Publishing Group Limited
Carmelite House
50 Victoria Embankment
LONDON
EC4Y 0DZ
UK

www.summersdale.com

Printed and bound in the Czech Republic

ISBN: 978-1-80007-439-2

Substantial discounts on bulk quantities of Summersdale books are available to corporations, professional associations and other organizations. For details contact general enquiries: telephone: +44 (0) 1243 771107 or email: enquiries@summersdale.com.

This book belongs to

....

In dreams, we
enter a world that's
entirely our own.

STEVE KLOVES

Contents

Introduction

Throughout human civilization, dreams have always been regarded as a mystery. We have them every night, and yet they are full of the strangest, most vivid imagery. What can it all mean? Just as quickly as they've come upon us, they slip away when the sun comes up, taking their secrets with them.

Some believe that dreams are a neurochemical process, whereby the brain fires random neurons, or attempts to sort and file memories. However, the prevailing theory is still that dream interpretation can have enormous value in helping us to resolve issues in our waking lives, and can be used as a form of therapy.

The mind has a way of delving into memories and experiences within our dreams that allows us to safely explore them, helping us to connect with the more hidden aspects of our psyche. By interpreting the symbols in our night-time adventures, we can apply the information they reveal to our daily lives.

This little book is packed full of fascinating facts about the brain and sleep, looking at how and why we dream, different types of dreams and their interpretations throughout history, and tips to help you remember them.

It also contains an A–Z of dream descriptions and their meanings, as well as all the information you'll need to understand the basics of dream interpretation. You'll find a handy journaling section where you can record and explore your own dreams, and put into practice the tips in these pages. With the help of some of the most prominent psychologists, sleep scientists and researchers in the world, this book will help you to pinpoint what your unconscious mind is trying to tell you, so you can sleep easy.

The anchor of
all my dreams is the
collective wisdom of
mankind as a whole.

NELSON MANDELA

Dreams Explained

Dreams are images, thoughts and feelings that occur while we're asleep. Our night-time reveries are usually made up of visual imagery, but all of the senses can be involved. Most people dream in colour, although some dream in black and white. Those who are blind tend to experience their dreams more in terms of sound, taste and smell.

Debate continues among experts about why we dream, and the theories about the role that dreaming plays include:

* Building memory: Dreaming may help us to consolidate memory and information for recall at a later date.

* Processing emotion: Exploring feelings in imagined contexts might be how our brain manages emotions.

* Mental housekeeping: Is dreaming the mind's way of clearing away detritus it no longer needs?

* Instant replay: Perhaps dreams provide a safe arena from which to review and analyze recent events.

* Incidental brain activity: Some believe that dreaming is simply a by-product of sleep and has no essential purpose or meaning.

Dreaming could be some or all of these things.

How often do we dream?

According to the National Sleep Foundation, we can have anything between four and six dreams per sleep. Researchers at the Lucidity Institute suggest that the shortest dream is at the beginning of a sleep cycle (around ten minutes), and the longest is nearing the end, when dreams can last for up to an hour. This is because our sleep patterns change during the course of the cycle and periods of rapid eye movement (REM) sleep become longer. During REM sleep, the eyes dart under the lids at speed, and the brain is as active as while we're awake. Although dreams are possible in any stage of sleep, we're most likely to dream during this phase, meaning that we dream approximately every 90 minutes, in line with each new REM cycle.

An estimated total of around two hours is spent in dreamland, although this amount of time can be spread throughout the course of a period of sleep.

Why is it difficult to remember dreams?

Although there's no definitive answer to this question, there are several possibilities:

* Researchers have shown that the thought processes we use to create or recall memories shut down when we sleep, thus preventing us from being able to remember most of our dreams, and allowing us to tell the difference between our dream world and reality.

* We may perceive the dream as nonsense or irrelevant; therefore, the brain filters it out. Jumbled fragments of dreams are harder for us to remember.

* We have lower levels of a hormone called noradrenaline during deep sleep, which primes the body and mind for activity. As it takes at least two minutes for the hippocampus to swing back into action on waking, this makes us a bit dopey. By the time we're fully awake, the memory of the dream has vanished.

Creative personality types prone to daydreaming and introspection are more likely to remember their dreams than those with a more practical mindset.

Those who wake more frequently in the night are also more likely to remember their dreams. Unfortunately, we're prone to remembering our nightmares, because any dream that causes a strong emotional reaction can jolt us wide awake.

How to improve dream recall

It can be frustrating when that idyllic dream of cocktails and gently swaying hammocks on a desert island slips from our grasp! To improve your chances of recall, try these ideas:

* Make a conscious decision before you go to bed that you want to remember your dreams, as research has proven that if you intend to remember them, you're more likely to.

* Research also shows we're more likely to remember dreams when we wake up in the middle of them, so if that happens, jot down what you can recall on paper. There are also smartphone apps that can help you to create an organized and searchable dream journal. Try focusing on the emotion of the dream, an image or a couple of words. Even a few brief notes will jog your memory the next day.

* Think about your dreams as soon as you wake up, before you "break the spell" by doing anything else, such as looking at your alarm clock. Keep your eyes closed and replay the dreams in your mind – you're reviewing them as you enter your waking state and this should help you to remember them.

Dreams throughout the ages

* Early civilization: Primitive tribes view dreams as either an indication of God's will or the haunting of the devil.

* 1450–1410 BCE: Dreams and their divination are referred to often in the Bible's Old Testament. In the Book of Genesis, the Pharaoh's dream of seven lean cows is interpreted by Joseph as a warning of seven years of drought.

* 1100–771 BCE: The Ancient Chinese believe that dreaming is the act of your soul leaving the body each night for another world, and that dreams imply auspicious or inauspicious things. The archaic and anonymous text *Duke of Zhou Interprets Dreams* from this time is still highly respected today. Traditional Chinese medicine relates dreams to the health of the body, and the balance of yin and yang.

* 2 CE: Artemidorus writes the first Ancient Greek treatise on dream interpretation, the *Oneirocritica*. The Romans and Greeks see dreams as prophecy, or revelations from God or the soul. Morpheus, the god of sleep and dreams, is thought to heal recurring nightmares.

* The physician Galen (c. 129–216 CE) writes *On Diagnosis from Dreams*, regarding them as important in both prophecy and healing. He diagnoses his patients through dreams.

* Septimius Severus (145–211 CE) dreams that he will become Rome's Emperor. When he succeeds, he recounts his prophetic dreams and has them recorded in the *Historia Augusta*.

* 1899: Publication of *The Interpretation of Dreams* by Sigmund Freud, outlining his theory that interpreting dreams is the gateway to understanding the human psyche.

* 1933: Jung publishes *Modern Man In Search of a Soul*, which sets out his theories on dream analysis and its practical application.

* 1950s: Neuroscientists discover rapid eye movement (REM) sleep and begin exploration of the scientific parameters of the brain in relation to dream production.

Psychology and dreams

Sigmund Freud and the interpretation of dreams

Sigmund Freud (1856–1939) was the founder of psychoanalysis and the father of modern dream interpretation. His book *The Interpretation of Dreams* was published in 1899 and is still in print today.

Freud considered dreams to be the gateway to the unconscious mind, and believed that it was only once you could distinguish between the *manifest content* of your dream (what a dreamer remembers) and the *latent content* (the symbolic meaning) that you could access your repressed experiences and desires.

Although Freud's theories have been widely criticized, due to his conviction that many neuroses stem from a sexual origin, his ideas were the foundation for further development by contemporaries such as Carl Jung and, later, investigators in the field of neuroscience.

Carl Jung and the collective unconscious

Carl Jung (1875–1961) was a Swiss psychoanalyst and the founder of analytical psychology. Although he often collaborated with Freud throughout his career, he diverged from the latter's belief that neuroses have a sexual basis and that the subconscious is "hiding something". He believed that libido is also generalized psychic energy, motivating us spiritually, intellectually and creatively.

Jung believed that dreams are a natural expression of our imagination and reveal more than they conceal, using mythic narratives and symbols to convey their meaning. He proposed the theory of individuation: dreams do not need to be interpreted, but rather their purpose is to integrate our conscious and unconscious lives.

Jung also believed in a collective unconscious, from which universal patterns, symbols and shared ancestral memories (archetypes) emerged. He reasoned that psychological constants in society, such as the need to belong and the need to be loved, suggest that all humans have aspects of a shared unconscious. Jung maintained that psychotherapists should guide the individual in creating their own personal mythology, enabling them to understand their dreams better and relate them to their waking life.

Calvin Hall and the content analysis system

Calvin S. Hall (1909–1985) was an American psychologist who specialized in studying dreams. He is famous for his cognitive theory of dreaming, which centres around the belief that dreams are a cognitive process: essentially, thoughts we have while sleeping. Along with Jung, he dismissed Freud's idea that dreams are trying to conceal something; in *The Meaning of Dreams* (1953) he writes that they are thoughts experienced as visual concepts.

Hall categorized dreams into five principal concepts: self, others, the world, penalties and conflicts.

In the 1960s, Hall and fellow psychologist Robert Van de Castle (1927–2014) developed a coding system, scoring dream reports against 16 content analysis measures, ranging from mythical creatures to emotions. A milestone in the scientific study of dreams, the Hall–Van de Castle Scale is still used today and allows researchers to analyze dreaming cognition.

Hall gathered much information from those willing to record their dreams and was a big advocate of dream journaling.

Ann Faraday and dream research

British-born psychologist Ann Faraday (1923–) was the first English postgraduate to receive a PhD in dream research and is considered a modern pioneer on the content of dreams. She is the author of the bestselling *Dream Power* (1972) and *The Dream Game* (1974), both about dream interpretation. The latter discusses the role of puns in dream interpretation.

According to the *Encyclopedia of Psychology*, "Ann Faraday... helped to take dream analysis out of the therapy room and popularize it by offering techniques anyone could use to analyze his or her own dreams."

The new dream interpreters:
J. Allan Hobson and the neuroscientists

A neuroscientist studies the innate brain structures in dream production and organization, while a psychoanalyst concentrates on the meaning of dreams. J. Allan Hobson (1933–2021), a Harvard professor and psychiatrist in sleep science, forged a more central path between the two.

Believing that dreams were a by-product of chemical reactions, Hobson disagreed with Freud's theory that they are full of deliberate hidden messages but agreed with Jung that they reveal more than they conceal.

In 1977, Dr Hobson and fellow Harvard psychiatrist Robert McCarley (1937–2017) showed how dreams occur. They suggested that they are not mysterious codes sent by the subconscious, but the brain's attempt to give meaning to random firings of neurons. Known as the activation-synthesis model, it was the first biologically based theory of how dreams arise.

Hobson and McCarley agreed that emotions could be a factor in dream creation, and believed that dream activity is our brain's way of processing information, ideas and experiences from our waking lives. However, they suggested that these meanings are only present after the initial neurochemical formation of dreams, and that activation-synthesis is the brain's "best attempt" to prepare itself for waking consciousness.

Hobson did much to popularize his work and wrote many books, including *13 Dreams Freud Never Had: The New Mind Science* (2005).

The future
belongs to those who
believe in the beauty
of their dreams.

ELEANOR ROOSEVELT

The Basics of Dream Interpretation

What are the different types of dream?

Dreams can take many forms:

* **Vivid dreams** are ultra-realistic, with clear or striking images.

* **Nightmares** are full of distressing content.

* **Psychic or precognitive dreams** predict something that goes on to occur in waking life.

* **Recurring dreams** pester you over and over again with the same imagery or theme.

* **Lucid dreams** occur when a person is actively aware that they're dreaming and can consciously control the dream.

How do I interpret my dreams?

Freud and Jung believed that dreams are the basis of your subconscious trying to tell you something. Dream dictionaries are useful, but so is journaling and becoming familiar with our own inner psychological landscape.

Ultimately, there's no objective way to interpret dreams and you should listen closely to your gut instinct – you're the one who knows what's happening in your life and who knows yourself best.

A small number of dreams may be prophetic, but most of the time they are reflecting something for resolution.

What should I look for in my dreams?

Symbols

Dreams are full of symbols, giving clues to your emotional state or drawing your attention to something in your waking life that you're not aware of. For example, a snake might mean temptation, or that someone's deceiving you. An apple may symbolize lust, while a bomb going off may mean that you're feeling angry about something. It's important to consider if the symbol has a personal or cultural meaning to you. A snake will mean something different to a devout Christian and to someone living in a Brazilian jungle.

Emotions

How does the dream leave you feeling when you wake up? Happy, angry, distressed? The emotion that you experience upon waking is an excellent guide as to your emotional state, and the meaning of the dream.

Waking up from your dream feeling numb may suggest that you're feeling detached from your emotions.

Themes

Do you often find the same themes cropping up over and over again, in various different scenarios? If you start to notice repetition in any of your dreams, it's time to think about the common message. Your subconscious is trying to bring something to your attention that is crying out for resolution.

Who is in your dream?

The person we see in our dream – whether it's ourselves, someone familiar or a stranger – will be reflecting something back to us about our own behaviour. You may desire the characteristics of the person in the dream, or see a behaviour that's telling you something about yourself. It's important to think about what the person in the dream means to you, and what they might be showing you.

Events

Do the events taking place in your dream relate to something in your waking life? Dream content can hide symbolic meaning but can also have a practical purpose, where the brain is potentially trying to process or consolidate memories.

Recurring dreams

Recurring dreams are more common than you might think, and are a sign that your subconscious is trying to flag up something really important. It may be that an unresolved issue, fear or behaviour is still plaguing you – or perhaps there are unexpressed emotions trapped inside that you've been so far unable to release. If a problem or situation is unresolved, you'll need to get to the bottom of it in order to halt these dreams.

Lucid dreams

Lucid dreams are a particularly interesting phenomenon, and their existence has been documented in cultures and belief systems throughout civilization. Some claim that during this state – used widely in yoga nidra and the Tibetan Buddhist practice of dream yoga – they're able to resolve waking problems, find the melody for a new piece of music or spend time with people they've loved and lost. Real-life limitations don't exist in lucid dreams – you can climb like Spiderman, blast into space, slay a dragon or meet the greatest footballer of all time.

Although humans have always experienced lucid dreams, the first scientific proof came in 1975, courtesy of Dr Keith Hearne and his sleep lab. The neurobiological basis for this phenomenon is still not fully understood.

Dream experts recommend the following to experience a lucid dream:

* Create a mental habit known as "reality checking". This means having more awareness of reality in your daily life – such as noticing your walk to work in all its sensory detail, or the lines of your skin – which in turn will lead to more lucidity in your dream realm.

* Before bed, set your intention to have a lucid dream and to do something specific, such as finding your hands.

* Set your alarm for an hour earlier than your normal wake-up time, so that you're roused during your final cycle of REM sleep. Turn your alarm off but don't open your eyes. Allow your body to relax back into sleep, while your mind remains active.

* You'll begin to dream again, while having control over your actions. Try to find your hands in the dream, and see if you can feel them by pushing your palms into the bed.

* On waking, record everything you can remember, including as much sensory detail as you can. Consistent journaling will generate more propensity to dream and, over time, will also improve your recall.

I've dreamt in my life dreams that have stayed with me ever after, and changed my ideas; they've... altered the colour of my mind.

CATHERINE EARNSHAW
IN *WUTHERING HEIGHTS*,
EMILY BRONTË

The A-Z of Dreams

In this chapter you'll find a handy A–Z of dream meanings, from Achievement to Zoo. Providing you with some solid clues on where to start with your dream interpretation, this dictionary explains some of the most common and baffling scenarios. It's always important to consider your own personal reactions to symbolism, as well as what's happening in your waking life, since that will also play a part in how you ultimately interpret your night-time adventures. Jung believed that there is a "collective" consciousness – that certain symbols mean the same thing to large selections of culturally similar people – and in this vein, this A–Z is a good place to start, with some of the most common collective meanings that could help you get to the root of that very weird dream.

ACHIEVEMENT

Congratulations! You'll be pleased with the outcome of a project or situation. The bigger the achievement, the greater your satisfaction will be. *See Graduation.*

ACTOR

If you dream of your favourite actor, you may desire some of their physical or personality traits. What role are they playing in the dream? How you perceive them, or the characters they play, can help you to understand the characteristics you'd like to see in yourself.

If you dream that you're acting, ask yourself: are you putting on an act in some area of your life?

ADULTERY

This one can leave us blushing! If you dream of having an affair, you may either have sexual desires that are longing to be expressed, or your dream could simply be a harmless release of sexual feelings or exploration.

Alternatively, your subconscious could be betraying you. Are you tangled up in a situation that's not in your best interest? Perhaps you've done something you feel guilty about.

To dream that your significant other is cheating on you shows your insecurities and fears of abandonment. You may be doubting your own value and feeling that you're not measuring up to others' expectations.

ANIMAL

Grrrrr! Animals in your dream represent your own physical characteristics, as well as primal or sexual desires. It's useful to analyze the qualities associated with the animal in the dream, in order to understand what it could represent to you. Animals can also signify the untamed, uncivilized aspects of yourself that you might be fighting to accept. If the animal talks, listen carefully, as it may drop some wisdom.

APPLE

Eating one of these tasty fruits in your dream is generally linked to lust and pleasure; alternatively, your dream could be reminding you to take better care of your health.

Apples also symbolize knowledge and prosperity, so if you see some growing on a tree, this is a positive omen. If you're picking apples, you'll reap the benefits of your hard work. *See Fig, Peach.*

ARGUMENT

If you dream you're arguing with someone, ask yourself if there's something you want to say to them in waking life. The dream is your way of safely exploring these feelings; in order to settle the conflict, you'll need to be brave and tactfully speak up. Alternatively, you may be feeling under extreme stress in some situation and your resentment is boiling over into your dream. Overhearing an argument denotes something you're unhappy with in real life. *See Fighting, Shouting.*

ARM

Noticing an arm in your dream can indicate your ability to love, give, take, create, defend or reach out. Arms can also represent struggles and challenges, and the effort we've invested in life.

The right arm signifies capability and your ability to create, while the left signifies your nurturing side and your ability to reach out to others.

Also, ask yourself if you need to "arm yourself" against something or someone, or whether you're "up in arms" and feeling angry about something.

AUDIENCE

Standing in front of an audience makes most of us want to curl up and disappear. In dream symbolism, an audience represents the world around you. You may feel under scrutiny or fear exposure in some way.

Alternatively, perhaps you desire attention or feel a need to bare your soul. If the audience is warm toward you, this could indicate self-acceptance. On the other hand, if they are unwelcoming, this may symbolize feeling uncertain about yourself.

If the auditorium is empty, you could be feeling ignored and neglected, or not being acknowledged for your achievements. Or if you're part of an audience, you may be objectively considering an aspect of your own life.

BABY

Aw! To see a baby in your dream signifies innocence, vulnerability or new beginnings. If the baby is smiling at you, this represents pure joy!

If you forget about a baby or leave it somewhere, it could represent an aspect of yourself that you've abandoned; perhaps you need to reconnect with your ability to play.

BIRDS

Birds represent your ambitions, hopes and desires, and if they're chirping or in flight, this shows that the sun is shining in your life. To dream of dead or dying birds indicates disappointments, whereas being attacked by birds could mean that you're conflicted and being pulled in too many directions.

BIRTHDAY

Happy birthday to you! If the birthday you dream about is your own and you're enjoying the celebrations, you're able to accept and even celebrate who you are.

If your birthday was forgotten in the dream, you're probably feeling lonely and underappreciated. Having a miserable birthday could indicate regret, or you could be afraid of getting old.

BLACK CAT

There's no need to be petrified of a black cat; they're erroneously associated with bad luck. To see one in your dream indicates that you're blocking your intuition because you're frightened to use it. In particular, if the black cat is biting, clawing or attacking you, then the dream means that you must acknowledge what your intuition is trying to tell you. So don't be afraid to stroke a black cat – it'll help you to get in touch with your instincts.

BLUEBERRIES

Blueberries are full of antioxidants, and their promise of youthful vigour may filter through to dream symbolism. Thus, they are associated with eternity and optimism. Alternatively, they could be a metaphor for feeling blue.

BODY

Dreaming about your own body signifies your level of self-worth, and this can be linked to how you feel about your physical appearance. The dream body also reflects your conscious identity or can be representative of the state of your health.

If you dream about a dead body, you could be feeling detached from those around you, or drained emotionally. *See Cutting, Face, Mirror.*

BOILING

Dreaming of boiling water suggests that you're in some kind of emotional turmoil. Feelings from your subconscious are surfacing and demanding to be dealt with. Something is "boiling over" or at "boiling point".

BONES

Oooh, secrets. Although bones in a dream might seem macabre, they represent the discovery of something previously hidden in a personal, cultural or family context. It could be useful to consider whether you need to get to the "bare bones" of something, or if there's someone you have a "bone to pick" with. Or perhaps you have underlying strengths that you've not yet recognized.

If you're burying the bones of someone who's still alive, this person knows something about you that you're trying to keep from coming out, whereas dreaming of broken bones indicates flawed plans or thinking that might require immediate attention.

BONFIRE

Like a phoenix from the flames, it's time to let go of old ways of thinking and rise from the ashes. Find a new path and move toward new goals. *See Ruins.*

BUTTERFLY

Butterflies are often a symbol of change or transformation, but can also signify romance, joy and spirituality. Alternatively, the dream may be pointing out a tendency to be "flighty" and highlighting your need to settle down.

To see two butterflies in your dream denotes a harmonious romance, while several butterflies could symbolize growth, inspiration and freedom.

CAB

Hailing a cab suggests that you need to ask for help in order to move forward in a waking situation. If you're travelling in a cab, you may want to question whether someone's "taking you for a ride".

CAKE

Just like in real life, cakes can be linked to pleasure and sensual satisfaction, though also overindulgence. Giving or receiving a cake is often a gesture of love and care, and if you're sharing the cake, you're able to give of yourself to others. However, not sharing could symbolize your need to learn to delegate your workload. Alternatively, you may be feeling that you're not getting your fair share in a situation.

If the cake in your dream is partially eaten, it could signify lost opportunities.

CAMPING

Dreaming of camping – or, ahem, "glamping" – probably means that you'd like a break, and preferably one where you can reconnect with nature and focus on the simple things in life. A campfire denotes a need for companionship and a desire to extend your social circle.

CANDLE

The light that a candle brings can dispel darkness and denote hope or a search for truth. If the candle is glowing, it signifies good luck. It may also mean that you've reached a place of contentment but have a burning desire to learn about the more spiritual side of life. A candle blowing out suggests that you're surrendering a significant part of yourself.

CAR

Dreams involving cars generally indicate the level of control you have over your life. If you're driving the car, then you're literally in the driving seat and in control of things. However, if you're the passenger, this signifies that you're taking a passive role in your life. If you're in the back seat, then your self-esteem may be low and you're allowing others to take over.

CHASE

Being chased in a dream is guaranteed to bring on the heart palpitations, and its general meaning is anxiety. To understand what your fears may be, try to remember who or what is chasing you, and consider the distance between you. If the pursuer is nearby, then you're feeling overwhelmed by a situation, but being a significant distance away suggests that you'll conquer your problems with ease. Watching the news or a scary movie before bed can also instigate these dreams. You have been warned!

CIRCLE

Ever felt like you're going round in circles? Your dream could be imitating a real-life situation and you may need to find a way to break vicious circles, so you don't get dizzy.

Alternatively, a circle in your dream can symbolize perfection, wholeness or completion.

CLIMBING

Climbing is often a metaphor for trying to rise above difficulties and achieve a desired dream, see a new viewpoint or gain a fresh understanding. If you're climbing, you're overcoming substantial struggles and your goals are finally within reach. You could also be rising in prominence. Conversely, to dream that you're climbing down indicates some hesitance and reservation. If you find yourself stuck and unable to move up or down, you might need to rethink an unrealistic strategy. *See Ladder, Upstairs.*

COTTAGE

An idyllic-sounding dream that often represents comfort, peace and simplicity; but it could also represent an altered sense of reality. Are you looking to escape your responsibilities and problems? If this is the case, you may need to take things one day at a time.

CRASH

Dreaming that you're in a car crash indicates a real-life clash with someone. There could be something preventing you from achieving your goals, or perhaps you've recently had a shocking or painful experience. Alternatively, this dream may be telling you to pay attention: it could be forewarning you of your dangerous or careless driving habits.

To dream of a plane crash can denote unrealistic goals, or represent your lack of confidence in achieving them.

CUTTING

To dream of cutting something signifies a broken relationship or severed connection. The dream could also be a metaphor for something you need to cut out of your life, or you may have been on the receiving end of cutting remarks.

If you dream of a cut on your body, identifying what the specific body part means to you will help you to identify what has hurt you. *See Body.*

DAFFODIL

These beautiful yellow spring flowers symbolize self-love, renewal, inner growth and optimism. They may be bringing you a fresh start of some kind.

Giving someone daffodils in your dream represents unrequited love: someone you're interested in may not feel the same and it may be time to move on.

DANCING

Joyous dancing in your dream can symbolize the rhythm of life: freedom, fun, balance and harmony. Dancing also represents happiness, grace, sensuality and sexual desires – perhaps you need to shake those hips a little more in your waking life?

Dancing with a partner suggests an enjoyment of intimacy, as well as a union of the masculine and feminine aspects of yourself. If you're leading, you're firmly in control of your personal life – or it could mean that you're being too assertive.

Dancing with an ex signifies your full acceptance of the way this person was and shows that the break-up was a positive decision.

Ritualistic or tribal dancing denotes your need to get in touch with your spiritual side.

DEATH

This dream is not as frightening as it might feel and, conversely, it carries positive symbolism. Death traditionally means change or transformation, and foretells major changes in your life, such as a new job, house or relationship, or a spiritual transformation within. *See Killing.*

DETECTIVE

If you see a detective in your dream, you may be seeking thrills and/or danger in some aspect of your waking life.

If you're being followed by a detective, you may have something you need to confess, or someone may be suspicious of your motives. Someone may be questioning you.

To dream that you're the detective indicates your search for your own hidden abilities and talents. Alternatively, perhaps you have a problem to solve or need to find the truth of a situation, so you may have to uncover your inner Columbo.

DEVIL

The devil is a complex dream symbol and could have multiple meanings.

A devil or demon can signify your fears, limitations and the negative aspects of yourself. Is there something you need to own up to in order to ease your guilty conscience? You may be experiencing an internal struggle, in the form of strong repressed urges or emotions that then present themselves as an external malevolent force.

The devil also represents intelligence, cunning and deception. The dream could be a warning that you're being deceived or unwittingly drawn into something that's not in your best interests.

DONKEY

Are you being as stubborn as a mule about something? A donkey in your dream represents a stubborn personality that's unwilling to cooperate with others. The donkey also symbolizes drudgery and indicates that you may be feeling overburdened or stressed.

DOOR

Walking through a door suggests you have some golden opportunities coming your way. An open door means that you're particularly receptive to new ideas, whereas a locked one means that you might be feeling shut out or overlooked. If you're locking the door, you could be closing yourself off from others.

DOVE

Most of us will have a preconceived idea of what these birds mean, and they do indeed symbolize peace, harmony, affection and innocence. White doves, specifically, stand for love, loyalty, simplicity, friendship and gentleness. The dove can also be a symbol of spirituality.

Nesting doves mean a happy, loving home life, while to see a dove fly away in your dream symbolizes a loved one who has passed away.

DROWNING

This dream can leave us literally gasping for breath, and indicates anxiety and being emotionally overwhelmed. Long-suppressed issues or feelings may be surfacing, and you may not be ready to deal with them yet. It's okay to proceed more slowly and with caution.

Dying by drowning in the dream actually represents something beautiful: an emotional rebirth. If you survive, a waking relationship or situation will survive the turmoil that you may be currently experiencing.

Seeing someone drowning in your dream suggests that you're out of your depth with something that's beyond your control, or you feel you're losing your identity in some way. If you fail in a rescue attempt, you should consider a situation in your waking life where you're feeling powerless.

EAGLE

The high-soaring eagle symbolizes nobility, freedom, courage and powerful intellectual ability. It's also a spiritual totem that denotes a strong divine connection and can represent self-renewal. You will tackle and achieve your highest ambitions and greatest desires with courage and determination.

EARS

Are you listening? Dreaming of ears suggests that you need to consider guidance from others, or perhaps there's something you're refusing to hear.

If your ears are painful, this could relate to hearing something bad or offensive, while your ears turning red symbolizes shame or guilt.

EGGS

Eggs symbolize fertility, birth and creative potential. They don't necessarily refer to a literal pregnancy, but they could refer to the birth of something new in your life, such as a business or creative enterprise. If the eggs are hatching, your ideas or goals are coming to fruition.

A nest filled with eggs is a portent of financial gain, while eggs that are cracked suggest that you feel vulnerable. You may be "walking on eggshells" around a person or situation, or you may be "breaking out of your shell" at last. *See Nest, Pregnant.*

ELDERLY

Respect your elders – they may be the bearers of much wisdom. Ask yourself: is the old person in your dream trying to guide you or help you with a decision you have to make? Think carefully about the person's behaviour, as this could reflect your feelings about ageing. If you see a healthy, happy old person, this suggests that you feel positive about growing older.

ELEVATOR

Up or down? In general, the movement of the elevator is a metaphor for the ups and downs of your life. An elevator going up could refer to a rise in wealth and status, or a higher level of consciousness, but if it's going down, setbacks could be imminent or you may soon be brought back down to reality.

Dreaming of being trapped in a lift could mean that your life is out of control, or perhaps you're feeling stuck in an area of your life.

ENVELOPE

Envelopes signify anticipation or opportunity. If you're opening an envelope, there's a message that needs to be conveyed to you, either by your own subconscious or someone in your waking life.

Alternatively, ask yourself if you're "pushing the envelope" in some situation and testing someone's boundaries.

An unopened envelope, meanwhile, indicates sad news or missed opportunities.

EX

To dream about an ex-partner or ex-spouse – whether you were kissing, fighting or got back together again – may be drawing your attention to similar behavioural patterns in a current relationship. You may need to apply lessons from that previous relationship to your current one, so as not to repeat the same mistakes.

Alternatively, you could be reminiscing about the good times that you enjoyed with a past love. Dreams of getting back together with an ex don't necessarily reflect reality, but they may be triggered by a change in your current relationship or could be helping you to see how far you've come since that break-up.

Dreaming that your ex has died symbolizes that you've laid their ghost to rest. Metaphorically, dreaming of an ex may also signify aspects of yourself that you've banished to the past.

EXAM

The nervous sweat on your brow as an exam paper swims before your eyes is a horrible experience. Insecurities, others' expectations and the fear of failure are all affecting your confidence if you can't read or understand the questions.

Alternatively, your feeling of being unprepared and out of your depth may mirror something coming up in your life that you don't feel ready for. Take small steps to build your confidence. *See Interview.*

EXPLOSION

It could be time to confide in someone you trust – if you witness an explosion in your dream, you're at risk of your suppressed anger blowing up all over the place.

FACE

Hey, gorgeous! Seeing your own face in a dream represents how you see yourself.

The dream can also mean that you need to face yourself, especially if you're looking in a mirror. Alternatively, seeing your own face can represent the external persona you show to the world.

If there's something wrong with your face, you may be feeling inadequate, while washing it indicates there's something you need to come clean about.

If the focus is on someone else's face, ask yourself how you see this person and relate to them. Or you could be experiencing a reminder of feelings or memories associated with this person.

Dreaming of someone whose face is blurred means that you have no real sense of who this person is and your subconscious is warning you not to trust them. *See Body, Identification, Mirror.*

FALLING

This is a very common anxiety dream, often symbolizing that you're feeling powerless in waking life. If you're not frightened as you fall, you'll overcome any obstacles with ease, but feelings of fear demonstrate insecurity and a lack of support.

FATHER

Dreaming of your dad or a father figure in your life symbolizes authority and protection, and suggests that you need to become more self-reliant and mature. The dream may also be drawing attention to your waking relationship with your father, or some aspects of their character within yourself. *See King.*

FIG

The ripe, juicy fig is often linked to sex, conception and eroticism, but it can also signify a positive situation. *See Apple, Peach.*

FIGHTING

If you're fighting in your dream, this indicates inner conflict that needs to be acknowledged and resolved. Conversely, you may be struggling with or fighting something in waking life.

To see others fighting in your dream suggests that you're not taking any responsibility for or steps toward resolving problems in your waking life.

If you're trying to fight but you're ineffectual, you need to work on your self-esteem and inner confidence. *See Argument, Shouting.*

FISH

A fish is an ancient Christian symbol, which can also represent conception or insights from your subconscious mind. A fish is a positive symbol, and eating it in your dream symbolizes spirituality, fortune and nourishment.

If you're cooking fish, this indicates that you're integrating new insights and knowledge.

Phrases such as "cold fish", "fish out of water" or something being "fishy" could shed light on a waking situation.

FLYING

Channelling your inner Superman can fill you with an exhilarating sense of freedom, and the ability to control your flight symbolizes how powerful you feel in waking life.

Soaring through the clouds like a bird signifies self-confidence and a happy state of mind. However, if you're struggling to fly or are dodging power lines, chimneys and treetops mid-flight, this symbolizes obstacles to overcome in your waking life, low self-esteem or unrealistic goals that you have set yourself. Dreams of flying can also denote a transitional phase in life, a desire to escape or spiritual growth. *See Ocean.*

FOREST

A walk in the forest signifies a transitional time in your life and suggests that you follow your intuition. Alternatively, perhaps you crave a simpler way of life.

Dreaming of being lost in a forest indicates the tangle of your own subconscious: you're trying to find yourself.

GARDEN

Dreams about gardens can often reveal areas of growth or change in your life. Dreaming of a lush garden indicates the eventual blossoming of your goals and objectives, while a garden full of flowers represents love and domestic bliss. If the garden is overgrown or full of weeds, it shows that you're neglecting your needs, and personal growth can't take place until you set aside some time for self-development. A focus on your front garden symbolizes what you choose to present to the world. *See Vegetable Garden.*

GHOST

This spooky dream suggests that you feel disconnected from life or are lingering after something unattainable. Thinking about what the ghost wants or what it's looking for could help you to get to the bottom of the issue. Ghosts also represent regrets that haunt us, memories of someone living or dead, or something in your past that needs to be dealt with.

If you see the ghost of a dead friend or relative in your dream, this suggests feelings of guilt in your relationship with that person.

GIFT

Receiving a gift in your dream could symbolize a talent that you were born with. Lucky you! Look for other clues in the dream as to what this could be. Receiving a gift could also indicate your generosity and how much those around you value you. On the other hand, if you give a gift to someone in your dream, you may be feeling generous, or you may need to express something in a way that needs to be carefully packaged!

GLACIER

Glaciers represent frozen or blocked emotions. You're likely to be shutting down emotionally and having difficulty expressing your feelings. If the glacier melts in your dream, consider this a good omen – you're thawing out and beginning to feel your full range of emotions. *See Ice.*

GLOVES

Gloves represent the way you handle things. Do you need to handle something with "kid gloves"? Alternatively, wearing gloves may mean that you're masking latent creative abilities that you need to express. The type of glove being worn in your dream may be significant: driving gloves may signify that you need to take control of your life, while boxing gloves denote conflict.

GOLD

Who wouldn't love this dream? Dreaming of gold, which signifies wealth, could be an auspicious sign. Depending on the context, gold may denote things that you treasure or value in your life. It can also symbolize spirituality, love, sunshine, inner resources and talents. Naturally, gold can also signify greed and corruption. Is there a gold-digger in your midst?

GOSSIP

We all love a good gossip... unless it's about us! Gossiping in your dream suggests that you're indulging in a pastime that's counterproductive. If you hear gossip in your dream, this signifies that you're trying to get information from someone, but be warned – it may not be accurate.

GRADUATION

To dream that you're graduating represents your achievements, and shows your successful transition to the next phase of your life.

On the other hand, to dream that you're not able to graduate means that you're putting yourself down and not valuing your accomplishments. *See Achievement.*

GRAPES

Grapevines symbolize wealth and opulence (not just a love of the old vino!). Seeing or eating grapes in your dream indicates prosperity and rewards for your fortitude, or they can be a symbol of immortality and sacrifice. If you're picking grapes, this signifies the successful realization of your desires.

HAIR LOSS

Hair is an important part of our identity, so dreaming of hair loss can be distressing. This dream does not actually mean that it will fall out, but it can be related to fear and insecurities about your desirability. Men who dream of losing their hair may be worrying about losing their strength and masculinity, while women who dream of hair loss may be anxious about their attractiveness.

HARBOUR

Dreaming of a harbour is a positive sign, indicating progress in your life toward new horizons. If boats are docked there, these symbolize dreams that will be realized.

HAT

A hat symbolizes the roles you may find yourself playing in your waking life. Are you hiding something from others? Or perhaps you are fed up with wearing too many hats and are spreading yourself thin? If you're changing hats, this shows a change in your thought process.

HEART

The heart symbolizes love and emotion, along with truth and courage. Ask yourself how you are currently expressing or dealing with your emotions. If you dream of a beating heart, try to remember whether the beats were strong and robust or intermittent and quiet – the former represents confidence in your choices and that you're content with your life's path, but the latter could mean that you're not paying due attention to what's really important to you. Consider the phrase "the heart of the matter": is there something you need to resolve before making a decision?

HEAVEN

This idyllic dream denotes your need for perfect happiness. You might be experiencing difficulties in your waking life that you long to escape from. This dream reminds you to keep the faith, and stay hopeful and optimistic.

HERMIT

This dream reflects either your loneliness or your need to be alone. You're feeling stuck and, as a consequence, you may be withdrawing from life and distancing yourself from people. Connecting deeply with yourself and with others can help you to find your way back from the dark.

HORSE

This majestic animal symbolizes strength, power and endurance. A black or dark horse could denote mystery and the occult, while a white horse signifies purity and prosperity.

A herd of wild horses running free in your dream represents a blissful lack of responsibilities, but if you're riding a wild horse, this could symbolize uncontrolled emotions or sexual desires.

A dead horse in your dream indicates the end of something. Are you "flogging a dead horse"?

HOSPITAL

These traditional places of recovery symbolize the need to take time out and heal. Gift yourself some TLC and some chill time.

HOTEL

A hotel in your dream is associated with a transitional phase toward new ways of thinking and being. Alternatively, you may be craving the temporary delights of a holiday escape, or undergoing some confusion, loss or transition relating to your identity.

HURRYING

Hurrying in your dream suggests a lack of preparation for a situation in your waking life, or it could also mean that you're feeling like a fish out of water. Alternatively, if your daily life is stressful and you never seem to have time to do everything – are you always in a rush? – this dream could be reflecting that.

ICE

If you see ice in your dream, this could mean that your progress is frozen, or you could be skating on thin ice. Slipping on ice highlights your lack of confidence or may foretell of an obstacle ahead. Falling through ice could be a warning that your emotions may come bursting through. If the ice melts, your negative emotions are thawing out or you're coming round to a situation.

If the dream feels like a happy one and you're gliding easily on ice skates, this may signify fun and laughter, or your confidence in life. *See Glacier.*

IDENTIFICATION

If you see your own face on an ID card in your dream, you're feeling pretty confident in who you are. If you lose your ID, however, you may be experiencing confusion about your identity. *See Body, Face, Mirror.*

IMPRISONMENT

The ultimate symbol of feeling trapped. Examine whether new ways of thinking or action can help you to move forward. Perhaps you also feel as if you're being punished for something.

INDECISION

Watching yourself procrastinate in a dream shows conflict. You're being pulled in different directions, or you're experiencing a lack of confidence in knowing your own mind.

This dream could be related to a waking-life situation, but listen to your heart and allow intuition to guide you.

INFECTION

To dream that you have an infection indicates suppressed negative thought processes.

For additional significance, consider the body part that's infected.

INJECTION

Ouch! Dreaming of receiving an injection seems nasty but symbolizes your need for protection or healing. Perhaps you're being injected with a new lease of life or some new energy. Is the person doing the injecting significant to you? Is the tone of the dream positive or negative? You may need to be careful what you're allowing into your life.

INSECT

In waking life, insects can be irritating – and in your dream, they also symbolize little annoyances. Is something or someone bugging you? More positively, insects can also represent hard work and productivity, as well as teamwork. *See Rash.*

INTERVIEW

Being interviewed in your dream symbolizes nerves and the fear of being judged by others. You may be taking to task some aspect of yourself that you're not happy with. *See Exam.*

ISLAND

This dream might sound like most people's idea of paradise, but are you feeling isolated? If there's no means of escape from the island, you may feel or fear being trapped in your life. If you're stuck in some situation, this dream is alerting you to make changes to attain your freedom.

ITCH

In waking life, we've all experienced itches that we can't scratch. If this turns up in your dreamscape, you may need to bite the bullet and do the thing you've been itching to do all these years. In general, itches in dreams suggest yearnings or irritations that need to be soothed.

JESTER

Dreaming of a jester could indicate your embarrassment in a waking-life situation, or be a warning that trivial or silly distractions will deflect your attention from something more important.

JEWELLERY

Dreaming of jewellery often reflects your sense of self-worth. Precious stones are associated with the qualities you treasure in life, whereas costume jewellery, or wearing too much jewellery, suggests that you're trying too hard to impress others. Your feelings of self-worth need to come from within.

If you receive a gift of jewellery, you need to integrate any corresponding qualities that it represents within yourself. To analyze this further, you'll need to think about the type of piece and what it's made of.

If you see an item of broken jewellery in your dream, this signifies disappointments. *See Necklace, Pearl.*

JOINT

Joints in your dream symbolize flexibility and the need to cooperate with others.

If you're having joint problems in the dream, this suggests that you're finding progress difficult and things don't seem to be working out as you'd like.

JOURNEY

Dreams of a journey often reflect your inner progress in terms of lessons learned and spiritual growth. Consider the landscape you see and the mode of travel for extra insight.

Alternatively, you may be seeking travel and adventure in your waking life.

JUDGE

Have you been up to something you shouldn't have? You're looking pretty guilty to me and you're afraid of getting caught! Alternatively, your dream may be asking you to make better judgements, or symbolizing your fear of being judged or criticized.

If you dream that you're the judge, you may be facing a difficult decision, or being guided to deal with something in an equitable manner. *See Jury.*

JUICE

This is one tasty dream! Drinking juice in your dream represents vitality and life force.

JUMPING

This dream indicates that you're willing to take a risk or make a substantial move toward a goal. If you find yourself afraid of the jump, perhaps you're being held back by a fear of change, or there's something that's making you feel unsure. Take note of how you perceive the jump. If it feels good, then something in your life could soon be making you jump for joy!

JUNGLE

A jungle is a mirror for our subconscious: the wild, instinctual part of ourselves. You may be shown aspects of yourself that are inhibited or perhaps you're experiencing turmoil in your personal life. If you're lost or trapped in the jungle, you're being hindered by negative patterns that you need to resolve in order to progress.

Any wild animals you encounter may be old emotions that need to be dealt with, so watch out for tigers!

JUNK

To see junk in your dream symbolizes the clutter in your life; you need to clear out old habits and ways of thinking, and you could benefit from both a literal and emotional spring clean.

JUNK FOOD

While we all love a pizza, tucking into some junk food in your dream may imply you're not taking care of your physical or emotional health in waking life.

You may need to re-evaluate your lifestyle and take time to nourish your mind, body and spirit.

JURY

To see a jury in your dream suggests that you're feeling judged and worrying about what others think of you.

Being part of a jury in your dream could signify an inclination to pass judgement on others. Perhaps you need to be less critical. *See Judge.*

KEY

Seeing a key in your dream could indicate access to new opportunities, knowledge or freedom. If you're locking something in your dream, you may be hiding away your emotions. On the other hand, if you're unlocking something or you find a key, you may have found the answer to a problem.

Losing your keys could mean unexpected changes or missed opportunities. Alternatively, you may fear losing your status in life. If you are given a key in your dream, you're being handed the key to your inner self and your own spiritual development.

KILLING

This dream has probably shaken you to the core and left you feeling awful. Dreams of killing someone are linked to anger, so try to unravel any real-life feelings of resentment toward your victim. You could also be attempting to kill off an aspect you don't like in yourself that's represented by your victim.

If you're the casualty, you could be getting rid of a habit or aspect of yourself that you're not keen on, or you may be feeling "dead" inside. Perhaps someone has "killed" you by wounding you internally. *See Death.*

KING

Kings represent status, achievement and power – this dream could be pointing out your excellent leadership qualities. Alternatively, the king symbolizes your father or a father figure from whom you may be seeking support.

Dreaming that you're the king represents either masculine power or that you've achieved considerable status and influence. But always remember that you must use your power wisely. *See Father, Queen.*

KISSING

To dream of kissing someone can reflect your feelings for them – either romantic or platonic. If this doesn't make sense to you then look at the qualities that this person possesses. Is there anything about them that you admire? Sometimes kissing indicates a desire for a closer relationship with these aspects of yourself.

If you see others kissing in your dream, you could be getting too tangled up in someone else's relationship, so back off!

KITE

Kites suggest high ambitions, but with the need to remain grounded. Persevere and your tenacity will reap the rewards. Alternatively, beware of a situation that could come with strings attached. If the kite is being buffeted about, you may not be in as much control of your life as you'd like. Kites are also a symbol of childlike wonder and fun, so grab life and enjoy it!

KNOT

Feeling a bit tied up? Perhaps you're in knots about something. If you're untying a knot in your dream, however, you may have the ability to solve complex problems and, if you persevere, a solution may soon be on its way.

LABRADOR

Labradors are symbols of loyalty and unconditional love. Perhaps you're the lucky person on the receiving end of these qualities, or perhaps you're growing your skills in this area in real-life relationships.

LADDER

Ladders in dreams can symbolize achievement or spiritual growth.

If you are climbing down a ladder, this suggests that you're turning away from your spirituality, while falling denotes difficulties. If someone is holding a ladder for you, you'll succeed with the support of others, and if you escape by using a ladder, eventual success will be yours. *See Climbing, Upstairs.*

LAKE

A lake in your dream is synonymous with your emotional state of mind. The lake may symbolize your tranquil inner landscape if it's calm, or emotional turmoil if the waters are choppy. *See Ocean.*

LAMB

This cute, cuddly creature is known to symbolize deception (consider the wolf in sheep's clothing). The lamb also signifies something vulnerable, pure and innocent.

LANDSCAPE

Landscape reflects the dreamer's psychological state. Is the land barren, strange and unfamiliar? Does this reflect loneliness in your waking life? A landscape that is teeming with lush, green plants could symbolize fertility and abundance in your life. Also consider whether the landscape is familiar to you – if so, what feelings do you associate with it?

LANTERN

To see or carry a lantern in your dream represents wisdom from within. You are being guided. Alternatively, there's some wisdom or knowledge you may be seeking.

LASAGNE

Food can often be linked to emotions. To see or eat lasagne in your dream denotes comfort, or it could be making you aware of your multi-layered feelings about something.

LATE

Dreaming that you are running late for a meeting or appointment can reflect your own lack of time management in real life or it could signify that you're struggling to juggle all your priorities. What event did you arrive late for in your dream? Sometimes not turning up on time can reflect your subconscious resistance to something or someone.

LAVENDER

This lovely herb symbolizes peace and tranquillity, or spiritual cleansing. Its appearance in your dream could represent your serenity in waking life, or perhaps the need for a little calm.

LAWYER

Dreaming of a lawyer indicates the need for assistance, and that you're being assured it is available to you. On a more literal level, you may be concerned about a legal issue in your waking life.

LEAK

Something leaking in your dream could denote loss, disappointment and frustration, and could indicate wasted energy on futile projects or a hopeless situation. Alternatively, your subconscious could be drawing your attention to repressed feelings.

LETTER

Receiving or writing a letter in your dream may indicate that someone is trying to tell you something in real life, or you feel the need to say something to someone. The letter could also be guidance from your subconscious. It may have been trying to tell you something for quite some time and now it has put its message in a letter.

MACHINE

Are you mindlessly doing the same things over and over again? Perhaps you feel numb. This dream may be warning you to break the boring pattern and get in touch with what you truly feel passionate about. Machinery can also represent your body, so take note of how well the machine is functioning.

MAGGOTS

Is something eating away at you? Maggots are often associated with fears of death, disease and decay. This dream is asking you to clear out your mental and emotional closet; confronting these fears will bring back some peace and stability to your life.

MARRIAGE

This is a positive and blissful dream denoting harmony or an important life transition. It could also symbolize the marriage of the self, and the unification of your masculine and feminine aspects. What are the qualities of the person you're marrying? They may be a clue to the qualities that you wish to integrate within yourself.

MILK

This wholesome drink is connected to nurture, nourishment and maternal instincts. Depending on the context, you may want to think about whether anyone in your life is "milking" you. Spilling milk in your dream denotes a loss of trust.

MIRROR

Mirrors are harbingers of truth, and symbolize the link between the conscious and subconscious. If you're looking at yourself in the mirror, you're thinking about what you see, or how you'd like others to perceive you. Are you contemplating some self-improvement?

According to superstition, breaking a mirror brings seven years of bad luck, but in the dream world this could symbolize that you're smashing an old habit, or shattering an old image and emerging as something new.

Alternatively, a broken mirror could reflect that you have a distorted or poor view of yourself. *See Body, Face, Identification.*

MISSING

If you're looking for something, this dream is telling you to take control; you're a bit overwhelmed by chaos in your waking life. If someone is missing in your dream, you may legitimately be missing them, or you may have some unresolved issues relating to this person. Are there qualities within them that you're missing or not acknowledging within yourself?

MONEY

Dreaming of money represents your view of your finances or self-worth and can be a highly emotive experience. How did the money make you feel, and where did it come from?

Winning or finding money suggests success and good fortune, or finding something or someone of value, whereas losing it alludes to a setback in your life or the loss of something that was once dear to you. From a practical point of view, you could be worrying over money issues.

MONK

Monks represent spirituality, discipline and inner wisdom. You're being asked to leave any negativity in your life behind and follow your spiritual path. The dreamer's own religious beliefs may further determine the meaning of this dream symbol. *See Nun, Spiritual Leader.*

MOON

The mysterious moon is often associated with feminine intuition, or hidden or "shadow" aspects of yourself. Seeing a full moon in your dream signifies completion, while a new moon declares new beginnings. A blood moon represents the end of something; a crescent moon denotes cyclic changes and rebirth.

MOTHER

Your mother showing up in your dream could reflect your own nurturing instincts, or indicate that you have issues to resolve with her, especially if the two of you are having a conversation. Alternatively, perhaps you are looking to her in your dream for advice.

If you dream that your mother is dead, you may be confronting the feeling that she is not meeting your needs in waking life in some way.

If you dream of being a mother but you are not one in real life, the dream is reminding you to show more of your caring side. *See Queen.*

MOTORCYCLE

Motorcycles symbolize the desire for freedom and a craving for adventure; perhaps you're trying to escape from your responsibilities.

MUD

Mud can symbolize the need for some kind of cleansing, particularly spiritual. Consider whether you are involved in some messy or sticky situation. If you're bogged down in mud, this suggests feeling stuck or oppressed by a situation or relationship, while mud on clothing can denote that you feel attacked by something or someone. *See Water.*

NAKED

Being naked is a common dream theme, and can signify feeling vulnerable and exposed in real life. Your naked self may symbolize who you are deep down; if you are comfortable in your own skin, perhaps nakedness represents an acceptance of your true self. Clothes are a layer of protection, so you could be breaking down barriers. Alternatively, you may need to show your vulnerability and let someone in. *See Underwear.*

NECKLACE

That pretty necklace in your dream could point to unsatisfied desires. However, it could also symbolize your wish for more influence over others. Lost or broken necklaces could relate to something that's lost or broken in waking life, such as a subconscious admission that a relationship may be beyond repair or that a part of yourself may be lost. You're being urged to have the courage to act on your gut instinct. *See Jewellery, Pearl.*

NEST

Seeing a nest in your dream denotes feelings of home, comfort and safety. What condition is the nest in? Consider how this could relate to your home situation in waking life.

Eggs in the nest could refer to your "nest egg" (financial security) but any cracked eggs in there could mean disappointments. *See Eggs, Pregnant.*

NIGHT

The depths of darkness indicate the murky depths of your subconscious. You may be obscuring an issue from yourself so that you can't see it clearly. You may need to do some emotional spring-cleaning in order to help it to surface. Alternatively, night-time dreamscapes can be connected with closure and regeneration from which something new emerges, or self-reflection. What qualities or aspects of yourself are you hiding in the shadows?

NOSE

Are you following your nose? It can help to identify a fine bouquet or lead us to a delicious restaurant. Noses are how we sense things we sometimes cannot see, so dreaming of one can represent your intuition. Noses can also symbolize energy and determination, and you may have your nose to the grindstone.

Also, consider your curiosity about something – or are you sticking your nose into a situation where it's not wanted?

NOVEL

Seeing a novel in your dream, or curling up to read one, may be asking you to look at something from a different point of view. Determine the genre and title of the novel for further clues to interpretation. If you're having new – novel – experiences in your waking life, the dream could be exploring these.

NUMB

If you're feeling numb in your dream, or a part of your body is numb, you're likely to be feeling indifferent to or disconnected from your emotions. You could also be feeling paralyzed and unable to move forward in some way. Look for clues in your dream – are you feeling cold or disconnected from a person, event or situation?

NUN

Nuns can symbolize exactly what you would expect them to: chastity, purity and duty. Or the appearance of a nun in your dream may be reminding you to keep a vow or promise that you've made. You could also ask yourself if there's anything interfering with your spirituality – are you too focused on material pursuits? If this is the case, your subconscious is trying to bring you back on track to appreciate the simpler things in life. Alternatively, a nun could symbolize your desire for spiritual connection or a need for meditative reflection.

   If you are a female dreaming that you're a nun, you may be looking to escape from unhappiness in your waking life, or seeking peace or spiritual connection. *See Monk, Spiritual Leader.*

OAK

Dreaming of this beautiful tree symbolizes strength, wisdom and longevity. Your roots provide stability to keep you steady and grounded, no matter what your waking life throws at you. If the tree is bearing its signature acorn fruit, this symbolizes your life potential coming to fruition.

OARS

Oars represent control over your emotions. If you're rowing steadily, you're doing a good job of managing your life in a balanced way.

If you're paddling with only one oar, you're going round in circles, unable to break a pattern, and you may need assistance to help yourself out of this never-ending loop. Alternatively, you may be on your own, without a partner, feeling that you're rowing without a mate.

OATS

Oats represent simplicity and comfort, symbolizing the basic essentials of life.

OCEAN

This magnificent body of water symbolizes your emotions, and represents the bridge between your unconscious mind and your waking life. Depending on whether the water is calm or choppy, the ocean can symbolize either a tranquil or turbulent state of mind. Dreaming of the ocean can also be a very spiritual experience, and may denote rebirth or rejuvenation.

The vastness of the ocean can represent your courage and your ability to weather life's ups and downs, or your feelings of empowerment and your realization that the possibilities of life are endless. Sailing on the ocean with the wind in your hair is a blissful sign of your feelings of independence and freedom. *See Flying, Lake, Sailing.*

OCTOPUS

Do you have your hands full in a situation you're struggling to get out of? Octopuses represent entanglement, and this could apply to a relationship. Are either you or your partner getting a bit clingy?

OFFICE

Dreaming of the office where you work could symbolize that you're taking your job home with you. Alternatively, an office could be reflecting your feelings about your value and your place in the world.

OLIVE

Eating these delicious Mediterranean hors d'oeuvres is a wholesome dream symbolic of healing and longevity. To see an olive tree or branch represents reconciliation, peace and hope. A crown of olive leaves symbolizes victory.

ONION

Onions are made up of multiple layers that need to be peeled back before the centre can be reached. Dreaming of onions suggests that you need to strip back the outer layers of yourself to find out what's really within.

If the onion is making you cry, this symbolizes that you're crying crocodile tears over something.

ORCA

These majestic sea creatures are appearing in your dream to give you spiritual guidance. They're inviting you to be more connected or to speak out about something. You're ready to deal with your emotions, and unite the conscious and subconscious aspects of yourself.

ORCHESTRA

An orchestra can represent your connection to others and to your own soul. It can symbolize the integration of various parts of your life and how they work together. A tuneful orchestra suggests inner harmony, while being a member of an orchestra could show your desire to fit in. If you're conducting the orchestra, on the other hand, you may be in control of your life, or perhaps you are seeking to control others – are you "orchestrating" something?

OWL

Owls naturally represent wisdom and knowledge. An owl in your dream can also be drawing attention to something lurking in your subconscious ("in the dark"), or it can be reminding you to use your intuition.

PACKAGE

If you receive a package in your dream, you may be receiving new information or anticipating that something exciting is about to arrive in your life. If you're sending or handing someone a package, consider what you're giving to them – are you transferring your feelings onto someone instead of dealing with them yourself, or are you offering them something nice? Or perhaps you're thinking about what you offer as a "package" – do you have an urge to express your hidden talents?

PAINTING

If you're painting in your dream, this symbolizes a longing to express yourself creatively. Take note of what you're producing – your subconscious may be "painting" you a message, guiding you to follow your intuition or uncovering some self-realizations.

Dreaming about painting your house could symbolize that you're smartening up your act for success. Alternatively, consider whether some aspect of your life could do with a makeover or if you're covering up something you don't want others to see.

PARALYSIS

This terrifying and very common dream represents feeling helpless or stuck. Consider where you might be feeling emotionally paralyzed and where you might need to express your emotions. Feeling paralyzed may also reflect the immobilized state of your body during the REM phase of sleep.

PASSENGER

Being a passenger in your dream suggests that you're floating along in life and not taking control; you're happy to let others make decisions for you. If you see other passengers in your dream, you may be expending too much energy on people-pleasing.

PATH

This dream symbolizes your current path in life. If the path is open and unhindered, your head is clear and you're making good progress. A blocked or winding path, however, flags up the need to pay attention to the direction you're headed in. Take a step back and consider your next moves before you act on them. Perhaps you need to reconsider something in your life, or make a change.

PEACH

Peaches symbolize joy in the simple things in life. Everything may be just "peachy" for you right now. The juicy peach is also a symbol of virginity and sensuality. *See Apple, Fig.*

PEACOCK

The peacock is an excellent omen, and denotes success, contentment and growth. Alternatively, you may be "as proud as a peacock". Consider whether you're being vain about your appearance, or arrogant about your successes. The many eyes of a peacock may be making you feel watched.

PEARL

Pearls can represent perfection, purity and inner beauty, although they can also symbolize tears and sorrow.

A string of pearls shows your willingness to conform, while pearl earrings ask you to listen to some advice, and a pearl ring symbolizes the purity of love. *See Jewellery, Necklace, Ring.*

PEAS

This small and abundant vegetable indicates the persistence of minor problems or annoyances.

PHONE

Is there someone you need to have a chat with in real life? Perhaps you need to reconnect or there's something you need to tell someone. If you receive a phone call, listen carefully to what's being said. If the phone is continuously ringing, there's something you're not paying attention to.

PIE

Perhaps you're finally getting "your piece of the pie" in some situation, or successfully sharing with others, meaning that everyone gets their fair share.

PREGNANT

Although this could be a dream that unsettles you, being pregnant in the dreamscape actually symbolizes birth or growth in some area of your life. Maybe you're ready to give birth to new ideas, or something fresh and exciting is developing in your life. You could also be frightened about taking on some major responsibility. Being taken by surprise and not realizing that you were pregnant suggests being in denial about something until it's too late.

   If you are pregnant in waking life and have this dream, then it may represent your feelings or anxieties about the pregnancy. *See Eggs, Nest.*

QUEEN

A queen symbolizes feminine intuition, spiritual growth and power, and can also represent a mother figure. A person seeing themselves as the queen means that they want enhanced status and power. *See King, Mother.*

QUEUE

Queueing is guaranteed to bring out the irritation and impatience in us; therefore, this dream is telling you to be patient. Sometimes you need to learn to wait for something, and it'll come to you when it's ready.

QUILT

This cosy dream is symbolic of protection and warmth, as the quilt fulfils our basic comfort needs. It may be made up of different patches and symbolize parts of your life making up a harmonious bigger picture. Analyzing the colours and pattern of the quilt can provide further insight.

RAINBOW

Seeing a rainbow in real life is always a heartening experience. Rainbows in dreams symbolize hope, success, joy and positivity. They can also represent feeling spiritually connected.

RASH

We've all experienced having to scratch that annoying, itchy rash! A rash in your dreams can be pointing out that something or someone is irritating you. Alternatively, are you bottling up anger or frustration about something? If you can work out what or who is bugging you, you may be able to think about next steps to sort the problem. *See Insect.*

RESCUE

Do you need assistance with something in waking life? Your subconscious could be crying out for help. If you rescue others or are being rescued yourself, you may be struggling to express a neglected or ignored part of yourself.

RING

Rings are obviously linked with marriage and commitment, but they can also represent completion. If you see a broken ring in your dream, it may symbolize the end of a relationship or a loss of commitment to a project. If you lose a ring, or it's been stolen, you're displaying insecurity in some matter.

ROSE

This exquisitely scented flower is most popularly associated with love and joy, and can also symbolize passion, harmony and femininity. For a more in-depth reading, consider the colour of the rose, as each has its own prescribed meaning. A red rose traditionally paints your dream as a romantic one; a white rose symbolizes purity or sincerity in love; yellow denotes friendship, but could be warning of jealousy or infidelity, while pink is the first flush of a new romance.

Withered roses signify the end of something, while taking time to smell the roses in your dream could be an indication that you should do the same in real life. If thorns are a prominent feature of your dream, this denotes thorny relationship issues.

ROTTEN

Dreaming of something that's rotten or decayed is not particularly pleasant. Your dream may be reflecting a rotten person or situation in your life. Have you done something bad, or are you wasting your potential? Or maybe you're feeling rotten – take care to nourish yourself properly.

Don't despair, because there may be a joyous aspect to this dream! You may be encountering a new stage in your life, where you're ready to grow from the decay.

RUINS

If you see some ancient ruins in your dream, they could be showing you an area of your life that's being neglected or falling apart. This dream is guiding you to rise like a phoenix from the ruins and find a path out of the destruction. *See Bonfire.*

RUMOUR

Pssst! Rumours in your dream are a message from your subconscious. Or perhaps you should investigate more thoroughly before you believe what you hear. Spreading a rumour in your dream shows your insecurities.

RUNNING

Sprinting away from someone in your dream like a champion athlete? It could be that you're trying to run away from someone or something that you're desperate to avoid. If you're running from danger, you may be refusing to confront your fears.

If you're running toward something, you're in hot pursuit of your goals or dreams, while running alongside a buddy denotes collaboration and mutual support.

Problems when trying to move your feet can suggest low self-esteem or could be a reflection of the temporary paralysis that occurs during the REM phase of dreaming.

SAFARI

This exotic dream suggests that you seek variety in life and don't like to be constrained by societal convention.

SAILING

Sailing in your dream is a general indicator of how things are going and your ability to deal with life's problems. You may be smooth sailing or travelling through rough seas, the latter denoting your ability to overcome life's difficulties. Sailing against the wind shows the struggles you're facing in waking life. *See Ocean.*

SALAD

A salad relates to your health or personal growth. Think about the positive things you need to have in your life for your nourishment and development. Eating a salad could also suggest a desire for nature and robust health.

A creepy-crawly making an unwanted appearance in your salad signifies worries about your health.

SAND

Sand represents a shift in perspective. Consider whether you're wasting time or letting time pass you by, particularly if the sand is falling through your fingers.

If the sand is wet, then you may be stuck in old beliefs.

SCAB

Scabs in waking life symbolize something that is healing over, and this is also the case in your dreamscape. There may be some physical or emotional wounds in real life that you're recovering from. If you can't resist the urge to pick your scab, you may need to stop picking at the wound and let things take their natural course.

SCAR

Seeing a scar – different to *Scab* (above) – in your dream is reminding you of something painful that has never completely healed. The damage done is still affecting your life.

You could be harbouring deeply buried insecurities that are holding you back.

SCISSORS

Wielding scissors demonstrates deliberate and decisive action. You're cutting something or someone out of your life. Or there could be something psychological that you need to remove, such as an old belief that's limiting your growth.

SHOPPING

Seeing yourself shopping can represent your options in waking life; you may even be aligning your identity with the choices you make. The store can also be a symbol of materialism, showing your need to keep up with changing styles and fashions. The type of shop, market or mall can give you a hint as to what this dream may represent for you.

SHOUTING

If you – or someone else – are shouting in your dream, this symbolizes repressed anger that's looking to find an outlet. If no one can hear you, it suggests that you're being ignored, or not feeling heard about something.

If the shouting in your dream strikes you as a bit demonic-sounding, something from your past is still bothering you. *See Argument, Fighting.*

SKY

A beautiful blue sky can mean a moment of clarity or life's possibilities opening up before your eyes. An overcast sky could mean that your judgement is clouded, or you may be feeling down about something in your waking life.

SNAKES

Yikes! This is a scary one that often has us waking up in a sweat. In general, dreaming of snakes is a wake-up call from your subconscious – you're being asked to pay attention to something important. Snakes are often associated with negative emotions, such as fear, and hidden threats, or perhaps something in your life that is unpredictable and out of your control.

However, if the dream has a positive vibe, a snake could be a harbinger of positive change, be it self-renewal, personal growth or transformation.

And let's not forget the Freudian and phallic connotations, where a snake is related to sexual temptation.

SPIDER

Spiders can symbolize feminine power, entrapment or a dominant female figure in your life. You may need to explore your darker, mysterious side, revealing something about yourself that you've been keeping hidden.

If you see a spider spinning a web in your dream, however, your hard work will pay off.

SPIRITUAL LEADER

If you see a vicar, priest, rabbi, imam, elder or other religious leader in your dream, you're being asked to think about your spiritual needs. *See Monk, Nun.*

SPOTS

A breakout of spots in real life can make us feel embarrassed and as though our imperfections are plain for others to see. Seeing acne in your dreamscape can show your embarrassment about not living up to someone's expectations, or even your own. It's time to be kinder to yourself.

TABLE

A table provides a sociable space that we can gather around with friends and family – so a table in your dream may symbolize conviviality or your relationships. If there are people at the table, think about their interactions, as these could reveal how you feel about your own relationships with others in waking life.

TALENT SHOW

Dreaming that you're in a talent show indicates a new stage in your life, awareness of your potential and the ability to maximize it. A cheering or clapping audience shows that there is a good network of people around you to offer support. If you're watching a talent show, ask yourself whether you're truly living up to your full potential or letting your talents go by the wayside.

TAP (OR FAUCET)

Taps represent the control you have over your emotions. Perhaps you have the ability to turn your emotions on and off? If no water comes out or the tap is stuck, you may be feeling sad or emotionally drained. Consider whether a person or situation in your waking life is depleting you. It's also worth noting the temperature of the water: perhaps you are blowing "cold" on some situation or relationship, or maybe something is "hotting up".

TATTOO

 Tattoos generally symbolize self-expression and a desire to stand out from the crowd, but they are also permanent markers of something, as they can't be undone. Examine the tattoo in your dream for clues as to why it might have special meaning for you, considering what it depicts and where it is located.

TEACHER

To dream of being a teacher indicates the passing of wisdom and knowledge on to others. If you're being taught in the dream, ask yourself what lessons you need to learn – are you still a student in some aspects of your life?

TEETH

Chances are you've dreamed about your teeth at some point in your life – whether they are missing, rotten or literally crumbling in your mouth (eek!), these dreams are very unnerving and are usually linked to anxiety in one or more areas of your life. Teeth can play an important role in how attractive you feel, so distressing dreams about them may be connected to fears about your appearance or how others perceive you. Alternatively, dreaming of teeth can be related to feelings of powerlessness. Is there something you need to speak up about? Perhaps you are struggling to express yourself, or you fear being embarrassed about something.

THEATRE

A theatre is symbolic of your social and public life. What does the performance reflect about your waking life, and how do the characters relate to any aspects of yourself? Are you taking on a new role in life, or being a drama queen?

THIEF

If you've stolen something in your dream, you may fear losing what you have. Alternatively, you may be trampling on some boundaries in a waking-life situation or relationship and metaphorically "stealing" from someone.

If you're a victim of theft, or you witness one, this indicates that someone is stealing something from you, whether it's your energy, time or ideas.

THREAD

Thread in your dream is a metaphor for your life path and destiny. It also represents the power to heal or repair, or a connection to your thoughts and ideas. The colour of the thread could also hold meaning, when interpreting your dream.

UGLY

To dream that you – or someone else – are ugly reflects aspects of yourself you dislike and that, consequently, you've rejected or denied.

UNDERWATER

Are you feeling overwhelmed in a waking situation or relationship? You may be feeling overcome with emotions. However, if you find yourself able to swim easily and breathe underwater, this is a good sign, suggesting that you're in control of your emotions.

UNDERWEAR

Your underwear is usually kept private from others, so if you see yourself wearing it in your dream, it may be revealing your true emotions. Are you feeling embarrassed about something? Or perhaps you are feeling totally comfortable in your own skin. The condition of the garments can also give an insight into what your dream might mean. Torn or dirty underwear can show a poor self-image, whereas beautiful underwear suggests that you see yourself positively.

If you see someone else in their underwear, you may be seeing their true colours, or it could indicate an awkward situation.

Or perhaps it's just time you invested in some new undies! *See Naked.*

UNIFORM

Wearing a uniform shows a need to conform or be part of a group. You may be giving too much credence to the views of others. The dream may be hinting that you need to pay attention to your own thoughts and recognize your individuality.

If you dream of a school uniform, there may be something hanging around that's unresolved from your school days. On the other hand, seeing people in mysterious uniforms that you don't recognize could represent a fear of invasion, or a sense of disorder and chaos in your waking life.

UPSTAIRS

Climbing upstairs in your dream can indicate spiritual or personal growth; perhaps you are reaching your goals. If some of the stairs in your dream are missing, you're currently missing a few steps in achieving your ambitions. If you trip on the stairs, you're not ready to confront repressed feelings. *See Climbing, Ladder.*

VACUUM

An empty space in your dream reflects feelings of emptiness – perhaps something is missing from your life, or you're not as fulfilled as you'd like? Now is a good time to re-evaluate your life and populate that void with positive things. You can start by writing a list of what you're passionate about, goals you'd like to achieve or activities to try. Hook up with some old friends who make you feel happy, or think about taking up a new hobby, expanding your horizons and meeting new people.

VAMPIRE

Is someone sucking the life force out of you? Or perhaps you're the one with your fangs out. Energy can be stolen from us in many ways, from small judgements and criticisms to outright anger. If there's someone in your life who's not good for you, think about taking steps to protect yourself. Alternatively, consider whether you're the one draining someone else.

VEGETABLE GARDEN

A vegetable garden represents capability and self-sufficiency. If you're growing your own food in a dream, you're able to rely on yourself, and you have all the skills within you to live a happy and fulfilling life. Remember to tend to yourself with love and care... and eat your five a day! *See Garden.*

VOLCANO

Something's about to kick off, and it could be you! Are you barely suppressing your rage about something? Perhaps an issue from the past is rearing its ugly head again. Volcanoes can be powerful symbols of transformation or a sign of positive things inside us that want to come out – perhaps you are feeling an urge to birth a new creative project, or there are new depths of self-knowledge just waiting to be explored.

VOMITING

Being sick in a dream can quite literally mean you can't stomach someone or something a second longer. Ask yourself what or who is making you ill. You may be trying to get rid of something that's been harming you, from negative beliefs to the way someone has been treating you. It could be time to run an emotional inventory, and think about quitting a job or relationship that isn't doing you any good.

WAITER

If you're serving someone in your dream, you may be paying too much attention to others and you should consider your own needs first. If you dream that you're being waited on, you may be feeling that you need to be looked after.

WALKING STICK

Don't be afraid to reach out to other people for assistance, as this dream indicates that you may be in need of some support.

WASP

This nasty dream could suggest that you're feeling tormented by something – perhaps things are tough right now, with conflict and setbacks permeating your waking life. Are you feeling "stung" by others' words? If you dream of killing a wasp, you're ready to stand up to whoever is attacking you.

WATER

Water is the symbol of your subconscious, and reflects your emotions and life force. Playing in water suggests that you long for more fun in your life, while boiling water suggests emotional turmoil. Calm, clear water denotes a peaceful state of mind and a deep connection with your spirituality. Muddy water indicates that you are wallowing in negativity or feeling overwhelmed by your emotions – you need to clean off the mud and give your emotions a spring clean. *See Mud.*

WHALE

These powerful spiritual creatures are a metaphor for intuition and awareness. Emotional balance is demonstrated by seeing the tail of a whale in your dream, while a beached whale refers to spiritual struggle. If the whale is dead, ask yourself if you've given up on a previous belief.

WINDOW

Windows generally represent your outlook and insight, so consider what you can see. If you're looking out, you may be considering the world as your oyster, or pondering a decision that needs to be made. If you're looking in through a window, you're going through a time of introspection that could bring you to a much deeper awareness of yourself.

A broken window could signify that you have a distorted view of life, or you may feel unprotected in some way.

WINE

A glass of vino symbolizes the good things in life: conviviality and achievement. Here's a toast to you!

X

X marks the spot! If you see an X marked on a treasure map, then perhaps you're on to something and will soon find your treasure. Alternatively, seeing an X in your dream could be a big no-no, signifying something forbidden.

X-RAY

If you dream about having an X-ray, try to remember which part of the body was involved – your dream may be pointing out a health issue that needs to be resolved. If you're the one being X-rayed, you could be examining deeper within yourself, either to sort out a problem or for self-development.

X-rays can also indicate that you should look more deeply into a situation or your dealings with someone. Look past the exterior to see what's really going on inside.

XYLOPHONE

A xylophone is a percussion instrument that is made with wooden keys. It can indicate concerns for the environment or the need for harmony and nature in your life.

YACHT

Yachts symbolize wealth and luxury, and dreaming of one can suggest either that life is free and easy or that perhaps you need more leisure time.

YARD

If you dream of a yard, it's important to think about the condition it's in and whether there are objects lying around. If any of those are visible, think about what the item might mean to you. Is it a ball or toy, suggesting you need to make more time for play in your life? A tidy yard reflects an organized life, while an unkempt one symbolizes something in your life that's out of control.

YEAR

A year represents the passage of time, so dreaming that a year passes could be showing you a cycle of growth. If a specific year is mentioned, consider what happened during that time for clues as to its significance.

YES

Yes! You've accepted something wholeheartedly – whether it's a condition, situation or decision. Or perhaps you're being given a gentle shove to go ahead and do something you've been having doubts about... Go for it!

YOGA

This dream could have multiple meanings – it could be reminding you to pay more attention to your body and physical health, or suggesting the need for a simpler, more spiritual life. Perhaps you need to take some time for yourself and relax more? Alternatively, doing yoga in your dream could symbolize harmony and self-discipline.

ZEBRA

Zebras in your dream can reflect your ability to see both sides of an argument, or indicate black-and-white thinking. Is there an area of your life where you need to be less rigid in your reasoning? The opposing colours of the zebra can also represent unity and harmony.

If the zebra is running, is there something frightening you that you're trying to escape from?

ZEN

Dreaming of being at peace with yourself shows your desire for tranquillity and simplicity. You may be feeling calm and centred, or you may need to take some time for yourself. This dream could be suggesting that you should dedicate more time to a zen way of living, such as doing more yoga or meditation.

ZIPPER

If you're undoing a zipper in your dream, it could mean that you're opening up emotionally, or to new sexual experiences. Doing up a zipper implies that you're shutting down emotionally – or perhaps you need to keep your mouth zipped tight!

ZOMBIE

Dreaming that you're a zombie may suggest that you're feeling "dead" inside or that you lack passion and purpose in your life. Dreaming of being attacked by zombies could be a sign that you're feeling overwhelmed in your work or home life. You may want to look for ways to inject more fun into your days, or perhaps a radical change is needed in order for you to feel alive again.

ZOO

Unsurprisingly, zoos symbolize a loss of freedom. Do you feel trapped or cut off in some way? Zoos are often busy and crowded places, so an alternative interpretation is that you're experiencing some chaos or confusion in your life.

Why does the eye see a thing more clearly in dreams than with the imagination being awake?

LEONARDO DA VINCI

My Dreams

The journal section of this book is here for you to keep a record of your dreams, making them easier to analyze and understand. Getting things out of your head and onto the page can help you to process your thoughts and make connections that you might not otherwise have considered.

In this chapter you'll find helpful prompts to steer you in the right direction and get you in the habit of analyzing your dreams.

This type of journaling can help you to decipher these messages from your subconscious, providing invaluable insight into your psyche and personality, as well as illuminating issues clearly for resolution. Once you begin to see common themes in your dreams, you'll notice that these are the common themes in your life. The insights you will gain can provide you with a previously hidden clarity that will help you to grow and move forward.

My dreams: An example

What I dreamed:

I dreamed I was a judge, scratching my head in the courtroom, when I realized that everyone was waiting for me to start proceedings. I kept taking off an eye mask I was wearing and had someone open the curtains in the courtroom. Once I started to hear the case, I was quite authoritative. I couldn't make sense of it and made up my mind that in the next one I'd structure the trial more, for example, by asking for a summary of the case first and hearing representations from each counsel. I didn't know who was who in the proceedings and I couldn't make head or tail of what had happened.

Type of dream:

☒ Everyday   ☐ Lucid

☐ Psychic   ☐ Nightmare

My mood the previous day:

☹ ☺

1   2   3   4   5   6   ⑦   8   9   10

What happened the previous day?

There was an incident where I felt judged at work.

Notable symbols or hidden meanings:

Judge and courtroom. Eye mask and curtains.

Recurring themes:

Fear of embarrassment and lack of control over my life.
Feeling out of my depth. Contemplation of justice.

What I think my dream means:

I think the fact that I was scratching my head at the
beginning of the dream while everyone was looking at me
relates to feeling judged and embarrassed.

The eye mask and curtains could relate to the fact that I
was having this dream after it was light and I'd fallen back
to sleep – I could have been aware subconsciously of the light
coming into the bedroom in real life. Or it could mean that I
want to "shed light" on and see the true facts of a situation.
It could be a fusion of the two.

Although I couldn't make head or tail of anything, my
decision in the dream to organize the trial next time and the
fact I was able to be quite authoritative show my determination
to get my own life in order.

Does it relate to anything that has happened in real life or something that's been playing on your mind?

I have worked in the field of law in the past, so it makes
sense that my dream would set itself in a courtroom scenario.

I have often felt judged, and the nature of what constitutes
wrongful behaviour is something I have been thinking about.

My dreams

Date:

What I dreamed:

Type of dream:

☐ Everyday   ☐ Lucid

☐ Psychic   ☐ Nightmare

My mood the previous day:

☹

1   2   3   4   5   6   7   8   9   10

☺

What happened the previous day?

Notable symbols or hidden meanings:

Recurring themes:

What I think my dream means:

Does it relate to anything that has happened in real life or something that's been playing on your mind?

My dreams

Date:

What I dreamed:

Type of dream:

☐ Everyday   ☐ Lucid

☐ Psychic   ☐ Nightmare

My mood the previous day:

☹   ☺
1   2   3   4   5   6   7   8   9   10

What happened the previous day?

Notable symbols or hidden meanings:

Recurring themes:

What I think my dream means:

Does it relate to anything that has happened in real life or something that's been playing on your mind?

My dreams

Date:

What I dreamed:

Type of dream:

☐ Everyday ☐ Lucid

☐ Psychic ☐ Nightmare

My mood the previous day:

☹ ☺
1　　2　　3　　4　　5　　6　　7　　8　　9　　10

What happened the previous day?

Notable symbols or hidden meanings:

Recurring themes:

What I think my dream means:

Does it relate to anything that has happened in real life or something that's been playing on your mind?

My dreams

Date:

What I dreamed:

Type of dream:

☐ Everyday   ☐ Lucid

☐ Psychic   ☐ Nightmare

My mood the previous day:

☹ ☺

1   2   3   4   5   6   7   8   9   10

What happened the previous day?

Notable symbols or hidden meanings:

Recurring themes:

What I think my dream means:

Does it relate to anything that has happened in real life or something that's been playing on your mind?

My dreams

Date:

What I dreamed:

Type of dream:

☐ Everyday   ☐ Lucid

☐ Psychic   ☐ Nightmare

My mood the previous day:

☹   ☺

1   2   3   4   5   6   7   8   9   10

What happened the previous day?

Notable symbols or hidden meanings:

Recurring themes:

What I think my dream means:

Does it relate to anything that has happened in real life or something that's been playing on your mind?

My dreams

Date:

What I dreamed:

Type of dream:

☐ Everyday ☐ Lucid

☐ Psychic ☐ Nightmare

My mood the previous day:

☹ ☺

1   2   3   4   5   6   7   8   9   10

What happened the previous day?

Notable symbols or hidden meanings:

Recurring themes:

What I think my dream means:

.

Does it relate to anything that has happened in real life or something that's been playing on your mind?

My dreams

Date:

What I dreamed:

Type of dream:

☐ Everyday   ☐ Lucid

☐ Psychic   ☐ Nightmare

My mood the previous day:

☹

1   2   3   4   5   6   7   8   9   10

☺

What happened the previous day?

Notable symbols or hidden meanings:

Recurring themes:

What I think my dream means:

Does it relate to anything that has happened in real life
or something that's been playing on your mind?

My dreams

Date:

What I dreamed:

Type of dream:

☐ Everyday   ☐ Lucid

☐ Psychic   ☐ Nightmare

My mood the previous day:

☹

| 1 | 2 | 3 | 4 | 5 | 6 | 7 | 8 | 9 | 10 |

☺

What happened the previous day?

Notable symbols or hidden meanings:

Recurring themes:

What I think my dream means:

Does it relate to anything that has happened in real life or something that's been playing on your mind?

My dreams

Date:

What I dreamed:

Type of dream:

☐ Everyday ☐ Lucid

☐ Psychic ☐ Nightmare

My mood the previous day:

☹ ☺
1   2   3   4   5   6   7   8   9   10

What happened the previous day?

Notable symbols or hidden meanings:

Recurring themes:

What I think my dream means:

Does it relate to anything that has happened in real life or something that's been playing on your mind?

My dreams

Date:

What I dreamed:

Type of dream:

☐ Everyday   ☐ Lucid

☐ Psychic   ☐ Nightmare

My mood the previous day:

☹   ☺
1   2   3   4   5   6   7   8   9   10

What happened the previous day?

Notable symbols or hidden meanings:

Recurring themes:

What I think my dream means:

Does it relate to anything that has happened in real life or something that's been playing on your mind?

My dreams

Date:

What I dreamed:

Type of dream:

☐ Everyday   ☐ Lucid

☐ Psychic   ☐ Nightmare

My mood the previous day:

☹

1   2   3   4   5   6   7   8   9   10

☺

What happened the previous day?

Notable symbols or hidden meanings:

Recurring themes:

What I think my dream means:

Does it relate to anything that has happened in real life or something that's been playing on your mind?

My dreams

Date:

What I dreamed:

Type of dream:

☐ Everyday ☐ Lucid

☐ Psychic ☐ Nightmare

My mood the previous day:

☹ ☺
1   2   3   4   5   6   7   8   9   10

What happened the previous day?

Notable symbols or hidden meanings:

Recurring themes:

What I think my dream means:

Does it relate to anything that has happened in real life or something that's been playing on your mind?

My dreams

Date:

What I dreamed:

Type of dream:

☐ Everyday   ☐ Lucid

☐ Psychic   ☐ Nightmare

My mood the previous day:

☹

1   2   3   4   5   6   7   8   9   10   ☺

What happened the previous day?

Notable symbols or hidden meanings:

Recurring themes:

What I think my dream means:

Does it relate to anything that has happened in real life or something that's been playing on your mind?

My dreams

Date:

What I dreamed:

Type of dream:

☐ Everyday   ☐ Lucid

☐ Psychic   ☐ Nightmare

My mood the previous day:

☹   ☺

1   2   3   4   5   6   7   8   9   10

What happened the previous day?

Notable symbols or hidden meanings:

Recurring themes:

What I think my dream means:

Does it relate to anything that has happened in real life or something that's been playing on your mind?

143

My dreams

Date:

What I dreamed:

Type of dream:

☐ Everyday   ☐ Lucid

☐ Psychic   ☐ Nightmare

My mood the previous day:

☹

1   2   3   4   5   6   7   8   9   10

What happened the previous day?

Notable symbols or hidden meanings:

Recurring themes:

What I think my dream means:

Does it relate to anything that has happened in real life or something that's been playing on your mind?

My dreams

Date:

What I dreamed:

Type of dream:

☐ Everyday   ☐ Lucid

☐ Psychic   ☐ Nightmare

My mood the previous day:

☹

1   2   3   4   5   6   7   8   9   10

☺

What happened the previous day?

Notable symbols or hidden meanings:

Recurring themes:

What I think my dream means:

Does it relate to anything that has happened in real life or something that's been playing on your mind?

My dreams

Date:

What I dreamed:

Type of dream:

    ☐ Everyday   ☐ Lucid

    ☐ Psychic   ☐ Nightmare

My mood the previous day:

☹   ☺

1   2   3   4   5   6   7   8   9   1 0

What happened the previous day?

Notable symbols or hidden meanings:

Recurring themes:

What I think my dream means:

Does it relate to anything that has happened in real life or something that's been playing on your mind?

My dreams

Date:

What I dreamed:

Type of dream:

☐ Everyday   ☐ Lucid

☐ Psychic   ☐ Nightmare

My mood the previous day:

☹

| 1 | 2 | 3 | 4 | 5 | 6 | 7 | 8 | 9 | 10 |

☺

What happened the previous day?

Notable symbols or hidden meanings:

Recurring themes:

What I think my dream means:

Does it relate to anything that has happened in real life or something that's been playing on your mind?

My dreams

Date:

What I dreamed:

Type of dream:

- ☐ Everyday
- ☐ Lucid
- ☐ Psychic
- ☐ Nightmare

My mood the previous day:

☹   ☺

1   2   3   4   5   6   7   8   9   1 0

What happened the previous day?

Notable symbols or hidden meanings:

Recurring themes:

What I think my dream means:

Does it relate to anything that has happened in real life or something that's been playing on your mind?

My dreams

Date:

What I dreamed:

Type of dream:

☐ Everyday ☐ Lucid

☐ Psychic ☐ Nightmare

My mood the previous day:

☹ ☺
1 2 3 4 5 6 7 8 9 10

What happened the previous day?

Notable symbols or hidden meanings:

Recurring themes:

What I think my dream means:

Does it relate to anything that has happened in real life or something that's been playing on your mind?

Look closely at the present you are constructing: it should look like the future you are dreaming.

ALICE WALKER

Farewell

Hopefully, this book has helped you to learn more about dreams, their content and interpretation, and the science behind them, so you are better able to probe your dreamscape and analyze your own night-time reveries to inform your waking world.

Go ahead and make full use of the journal section of this book – it will help you to develop excellent habits when it comes to recording your dreams, fostering your fascination with them and allowing you to connect with your innermost self. Listening to messages from our subconscious can improve our day-to-day life experience and put us in touch with what we're really feeling.

Sweet dreams!

Index of Dreams

Landscape 70
Lantern 70
Lasagne 71
Late 71
Lavender 71
Lawyer 72
Leak 72
Letter 72
Machine 73
Maggots 73
Marriage 73
Milk 74
Mirror 74
Missing 74
Money 75
Monk 75
Moon 75
Mother 76
Motorcycle 76
Mud 76
Naked 77
Necklace 77
Nest 78
Night 78
Nose 79
Novel 79
Numb 80
Nun 80
Oak 81
Oars 81
Oats 81
Ocean 82
Octopus 82
Office 83
Olive 83
Onion 83
Orca 84
Orchestra 84
Owl 84

Package 85
Painting 85
Paralysis 86
Passenger 86
Path 86
Peach 87
Peacock 87
Pearl 87
Peas 87
Phone 88
Pie 88
Pregnant 88
Queen 89
Queue 89
Quilt 89
Rainbow 90
Rash 90
Rescue 90
Ring 90
Rose 91
Rotten 91
Ruins 92
Rumour 92
Running 92
Safari 93
Sailing 93
Salad 93
Sand 94
Scab 94
Scar 94
Scissors 95
Shopping 95
Shouting 95
Sky 96
Snakes 96
Spider 97
Spiritual Leader 97
Spots 97
Table 98

Talent Show 98
Tap (or Faucet) 98
Tattoo 99
Teacher 99
Teeth 99
Theatre 100
Thief 100
Thread 100
Ugly 101
Underwater 101
Underwear 101
Uniform 102
Upstairs 102
Vacuum 103
Vampire 103
Vegetable Garden 103
Volcano 104
Vomiting 104
Waiter 105
Walking Stick 105
Wasp 105
Water 105
Whale 106
Window 106
Wine 106
X 107
X-Ray 107
Xylophone 107
Yacht 108
Yard 108
Year 108
Yes 109
Yoga 109
Zebra 110
Zen 110
Zipper 110
Zombie 111
Zoo 111

Have you enjoyed this book? If so, find us
on Facebook at **Summersdale Publishers**,
on Twitter at **@Summersdale** and on
Instagram at **@summersdalebooks** and get
in touch. We'd love to hear from you!

www.summersdale.com

Image Credits